Our Living World

Every day we see many living things—human beings, cats, dogs, insects, trees and so on. What are they made of, and how do they manage to live? How does one kind help or hinder another, how did they come into existence and how have they changed in the course of hundreds of millions of years?

This book gives answers to these and other questions about living things. Francis Jackson tells of the ways of life of a number of animals and plants, large and small, and how they get energy to grow and do work.

Here is an outline history of the world of life, in clear simple text, with equally clear and attractive illustrations.

Finding Out About SCIENCE

Edited by
KURT ROWLAND

OUR LIVING WORLD

By FRANCIS JACKSON

Illustrated by GAYNOR CHAPMAN
and LASZLO ACS

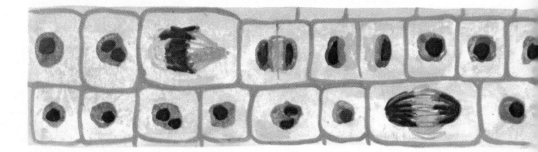

Golden Press 🦅 New York

THIS EDITION PUBLISHED 1966 BY GOLDEN PRESS, INC., NEW YORK.

Copyright © 1964 by The John Day Company Inc. and Weidenfeld & Nicolson (Educational) Ltd. All rights reserved. This book, or parts thereof, must not be reproduced in any form without permission. This edition printed in the U.S.A. by Western Printing and Lithographing Company.

Library of Congress Catalog
Card Number 64-10016

ACKNOWLEDGMENTS

The photograph at the top of page 11 is reproduced by courtesy of the Wellcome Foundation Ltd., London, and the one on page 28 is by courtesy of Friedrich Reinhardt Ag., Basle

Contents

When we look at the world around us we see some things that we regard as living, for instance, trees, birds and flowers, and others, such as rocks, nails and glass, which we call non-living. We would all agree that a rock, for instance, is not alive, but in what way is it different from a beetle or a tree or an elephant?

6

Living things can produce others like themselves, that is, they reproduce. Human beings have babies, cats have kittens and dogs puppies, but a rock does not reproduce in this way. Also, in order to carry on their activities, living things must have energy and this they get from their surroundings.

Energy is the ability to do work. The energy that drives a car along comes from burning gasoline in the engine, and it is sometimes said that living things get energy by *burning* food. The living thing—or *organism*, as we call it—"burns" its food in a series of short steps, and not in one great flash.

The body, like a car, gets its energy from the fuel it uses. In a car the energy is released in the engine; in the human body it is released in the cells

7

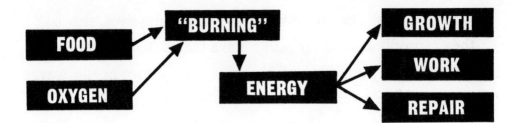

In this way, an organism gets energy from food without the need to reach high temperatures like those of running car engines. It does this by means of special proteins called *enzymes*. An engine uses fuel only for work, but the organism turns some of its food into part of itself, so it will grow, or repair worn-out parts. We, like most living things, use oxygen from the air to help us "burn" our foods. Some organisms, mostly so small that they are visible only through microscopes, can live without breathing oxygen, but they do not change their food into energy quite so well as those organisms which use oxygen.

It can be shown in the laboratory that more oxygen is used when the boy is pedalling than when he is still

The whole world, living and non-living, consists of different chemical elements, such as oxygen, hydrogen, carbon and nitrogen. The smallest particles, the *atoms*, of these elements join up in various ways to form *molecules*. In living things these molecules, the stuff of which they are made, are very large and complicated; we could say they are parts of the "machines" which carry on the processes necessary for living. Some of these substances are household words—fats, *proteins* and *carbohydrates*. You are probably familiar with fats; proteins are meaty substances but are also found in plants; sugars, starch and other substances are carbohydrates.

So you see that there are no special elements or atoms in living things, that is to say, they are made of the same atoms as non-living things. The secret of life lies in the special arrangement of a number of ordinary atoms.

FATS

CARBOHYDRATES

PROTEINS

In everyday life, we look at things with our unaided eyes, but the *microscope* can reveal a whole new world to us. One of the first men to use microscopes was a Dutchman, Anthony van Leeuwenhoek, who lived in Delft from 1632 to 1723. With the aid of simple, high-quality lenses which he made himself, he discovered that there were many tiny living things in water and other materials. Leeuwenhoek was the first man to see these small creatures, including what we now call *protozoa* and *bacteria*, and gave the first description of red blood cells.

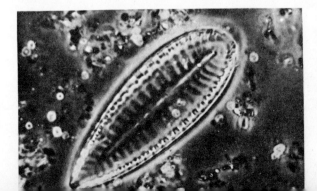

Living things in a drop of water, such as Leeuwenhoek might have seen through his microscope. The large object in the middle of the picture is a microscopic plant

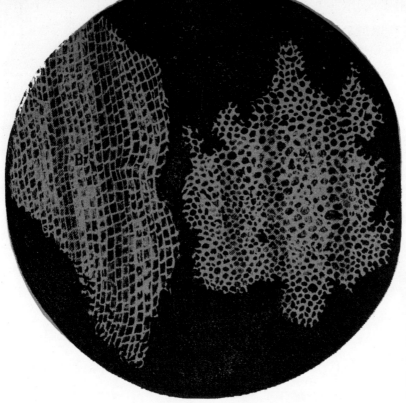

(*Left*) Hooke's drawing of 1665, showing the cell structure of cork. This was the first time the cells of a plant had been shown

In 1665, the scientist Robert Hooke looked through a microscope at some thin slices of cork. He saw that the cork was apparently made of tiny "boxes" packed together, and he called these cells, from the Latin word meaning "a small room". In the early nineteenth century it was found that plants and animals consist of cells, which can be seen through the microscope. Plant cells have thick, stiff walls made of a carbohydrate, *cellulose*, and they can therefore be seen more easily than animal cells.

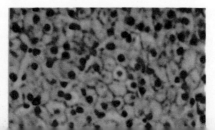

Photomicrographs of plant cells (*left*) and animal cells (*right*)

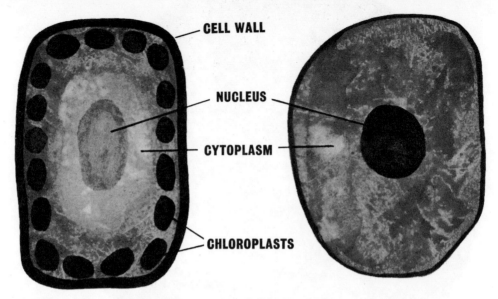

CELL WALL

NUCLEUS

CYTOPLASM

CHLOROPLASTS

The cell is the smallest unit of life and if we are to understand how living things work, we must take a closer look at the cell. A typical cell consists of a jelly-like substance called *protoplasm*. It contains a dense center—or *nucleus*—which controls the cell. The rest of the cell's substance is called *cytoplasm*. In the cytoplasm we find various grain-like and thread-like objects, all of them able to carry out some of the important jobs necessary for living.

An important difference between plant cells and animal cells lies in the *chloroplasts* which are found only in plant cells. These chloroplasts, which are green because they contain a green coloring matter, or pigment, called *chlorophyll*, are one of the marvels of the living world. By means of chloroplasts, the plant traps sunlight and uses the energy of light to build up sugars and other chemicals from carbon

The plant traps the energy from the sun in its leaves

dioxide and water. When the plant changes these simple substances into more complicated ones, some oxygen, from the water, is left over, and this is given off into the atmosphere. In this way, plants lock up energy from the sun in the large molecules which they form, and at the same time enrich the air with oxygen. The process by which the plants use light energy to build up large molecules from small ones is called *photosynthesis*, which is a Greek word meaning "a building up by means of light".

Because plants need sunlight for photosynthesis, they will always grow toward the light

Not all animals eat plants. Some use other, smaller animals for food, which in turn eat still smaller ones. But the first animal of such a chain must live on plants because all our energy comes from sunlight and only plants can use this form of energy.

Now we are beginning to understand how the animal world and plant world work together. The sun shines from the sky, and in the fields and seas plants use the energy of its light to help them grow. Man and other animals eat the plants, and so "feed" on the sun's energy, and this enables them to work. Man and animals use oxygen to burn the foods they obtain from plants, and breathe out carbon dioxide which returns to the air where plants can use it again. Plants use some oxygen, but in photosynthesis produce more than they require, so the oxygen of the air is continuously added to by plants.

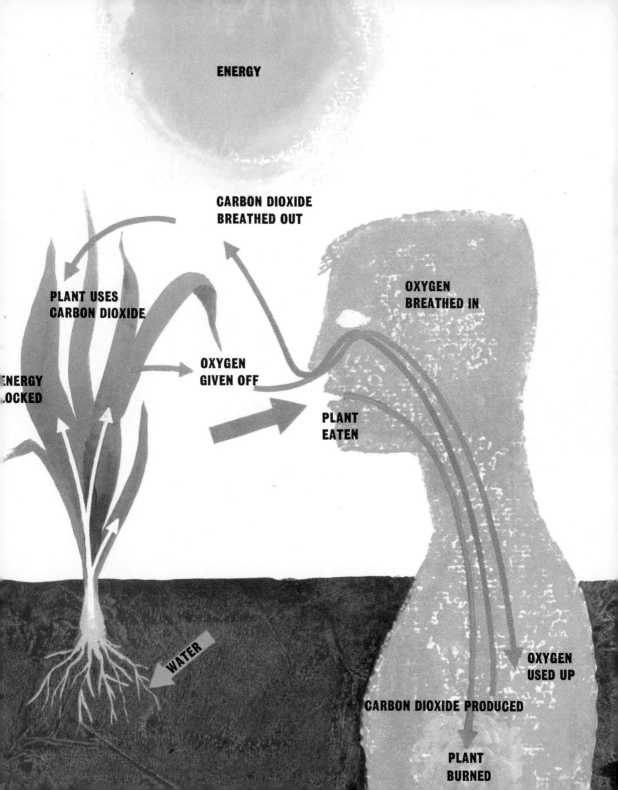

One of Leeuwenhoek's microscopes. He looked through the tiny lens in the plate. The object to be magnified was fixed to the fine point and its position could be adjusted by turning the screws

Hooke's compound microscope

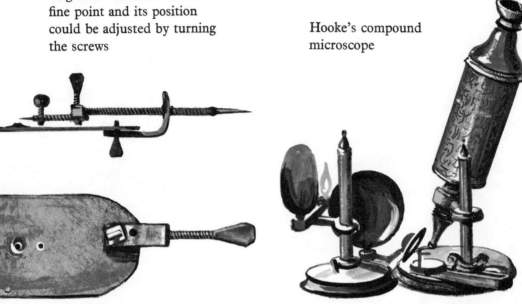

The microscopes made and used by Leeuwenhoek were simple instruments, consisting of a single lens. Hooke used a *compound microscope*, that is to say, one consisting of more than one lens. A good compound microscope will show details which are only 1/2000 of a millimeter across in the original object. To show up smaller details, the scientist uses an *electron microscope*. Photographs can be obtained which show the object very highly magnified—even many hundreds of thousands times longer and broader than it is in reality.

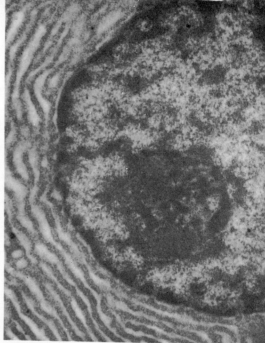

The photograph above shows part of a stomach cell magnified 37,000 times its actual size. It was taken through a modern electron microscope like the one on the left

There are some inexpensive compound microscopes to be bought in toyshops. If you want to see something of living things under the microscope for yourself, you will find one of these sufficient to start you off on your discoveries. You will also need some glass slides to carry the objects you examine.

Water containing slime or scum from a pond contains many plants and animals so small that they can be seen only under the microscope—they are called *microscopic* organisms. Even a single drop of pond water will show many different living things.

You can repeat Hooke's observation on cork. Take a cork, and with a sharp razor blade in a safe holder, shave off the thinnest slice you can cut, place it on a glass slide and look at this through the microscope. The spaces formerly filled by cell contents are easily seen. You can do the same with the stem of a cut flower.

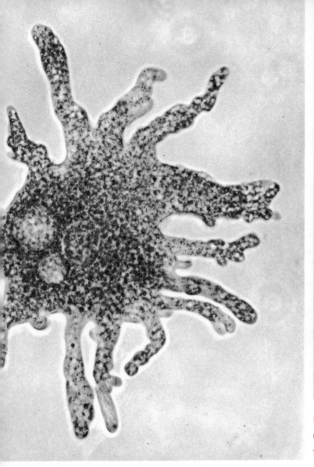
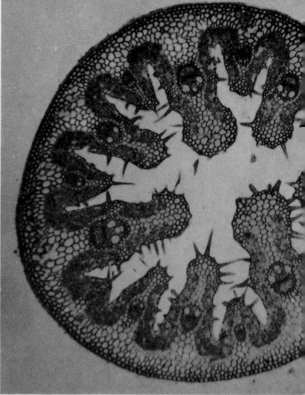

(*Left*) An amoeba, and
(*right*) a section through
the leaf of a marram grass

Some of the organisms visible through microscopes
consist of only a single cell. An example is the *amoeba*. The
largest amoebae are about a millimeter across, but other kinds
are smaller. The amoeba, which lives in water, mud and damp
soil, moves by thrusting out a part of itself and "flowing"
along, so that the rest of the animal seems to flow into and
swell up the part that was pushed out. In the soft-bodied
amoeba, there is a nucleus and cytoplasm, as in other
typical cells.

19

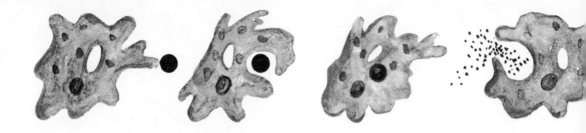

The amoeba feeds by surrounding food particles which come into contact with it. It flows around its food, which then lies in a sort of "bubble" within the animal. Here the food is digested, that is, it is changed into materials which will dissolve in water and pass into the rest of the cell. The amoeba simply flows away from any waste material it could not digest, and leaves it behind.

Like other living things, the amoeba reproduces its kind. When it has reached a certain size, it splits into two. The nucleus and cytoplasm divide, so that where there was formerly one animal, there are now two.

The amoeba is a microscopic animal. There are many other microscopic animals, and there are also microscopic plants, many of which are single-celled. Microscopic plants have chloroplasts, and carry on photosynthesis. The countless billions of these plants in the seas of the world together account for about four fifths of all the photosynthesis on the Earth.

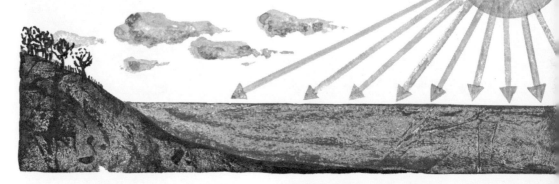

Some microscopic organisms combine features of plants and animals. Euglena is an example. It has chloroplasts, and can live like a plant in the light. It is also able to live on foods of the kind required by animals, so it is difficult for us to decide whether to call Euglena a plant or an animal.

A euglena

There is a great range in size between the smallest and largest living organisms. At one end of the scale we have bacteria a few thousandths of a millimeter long. At the other end are organisms such as the blue whale, the largest animal, as much as 100 feet long and 120 tons in weight. The largest trees may reach 350 feet in height. These large organisms are vast collections of precisely arranged cells.

A blue whale

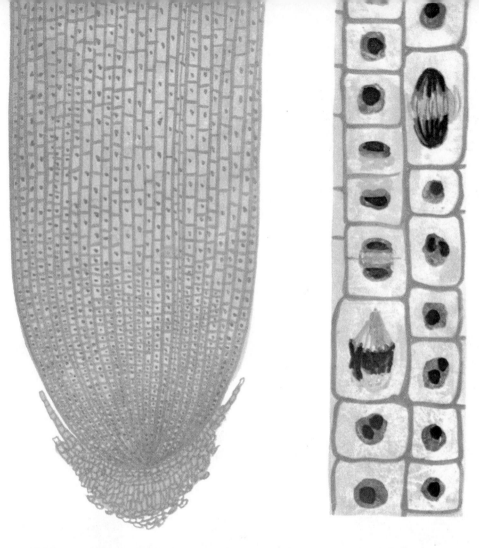

This magnified picture of the tip of a growing root shows how an organism consisting of many cells is formed. The cells split and produce new cells, which do not separate as in the dividing amoeba, but remain stuck together. In the still more magnified picture on the right, cells can be seen in the process of splitting.

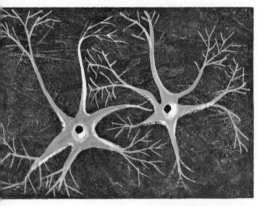

NERVE CELLS

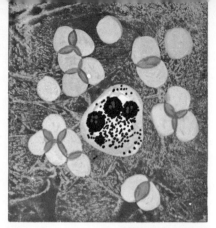

BLOOD CELLS

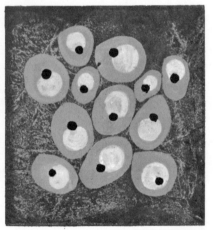

FAT CELLS

BONE CELLS

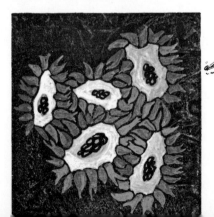

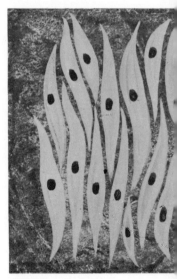

MUSCLE CELLS

Some of the different cells which are found in the human body. Each one has its special purpose

In the amoeba, one cell behaves as a complete animal, moving, growing, reproducing, digesting food, and generally carrying out all the changes necessary for living. In a more complicated organism, such as man, there are different types of cell, each type forming a *tissue* with special jobs to perform. The body is supported by a *skeleton* of bones which are made up of hard tough substances produced by special cells. The movements of the body are produced by muscles, and these consist of collections of cells which are especially good at contracting powerfully. The skin, which is a tissue of tough, hard-wearing cells, acts as a protective covering for the body.

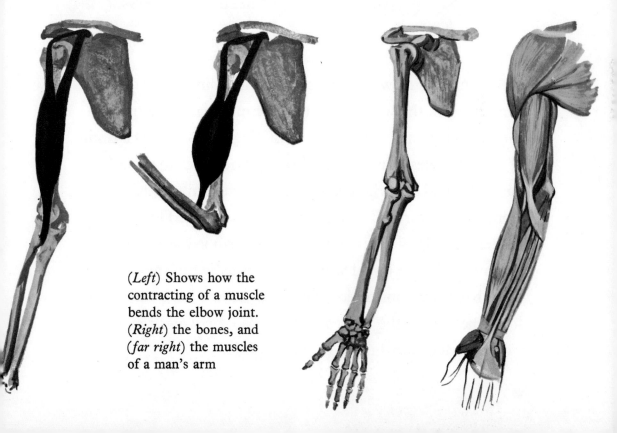

(*Left*) Shows how the contracting of a muscle bends the elbow joint. (*Right*) the bones, and (*far right*) the muscles of a man's arm

Water moves up and down a tree through tiny tubes. (*Above*) A slice through a tree trunk, showing some of the tubes magnified

A plant obtains water, mineral salts and simple chemicals from the soil; the water bearing these materials rises up through very fine tubes in the stem. Sugars formed as a result of photosynthesis are carried through fine tubes to other parts of the plant, where they can be turned into starch and stored in this form. The transport system needed by the higher animals, such as fish, frogs and man is more complicated. The blood which is continually pumped by the heart has many jobs to do. It must distribute food and oxygen to all the cells of the body and must also carry away many waste products, including carbon dioxide.

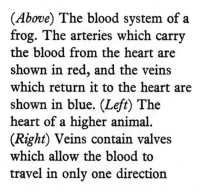

(*Above*) The blood system of a frog. The arteries which carry the blood from the heart are shown in red, and the veins which return it to the heart are shown in blue. (*Left*) The heart of a higher animal. (*Right*) Veins contain valves which allow the blood to travel in only one direction

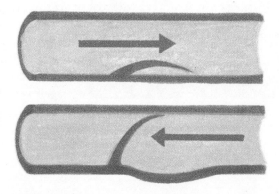

We have seen that the cells of the many-celled organisms have to carry out different jobs, and some sort of control is needed to make sure that each part of the body acts properly at the right time. This is what the central nervous system is for. It consists of the brain and nerves which go out to all parts of the body and connect the cells of the brain with other cells of the body. Certain parts of the brain are responsible for different activities. By means of our eyes, ears

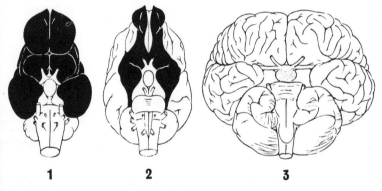

1   2   3

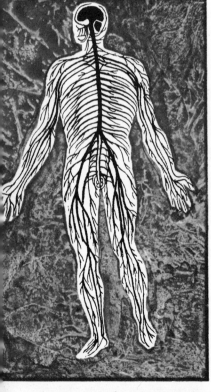

Man's central nervous system

(*Above*) 1 shows the brain of an armadillo, 2 the brain of a dog, 3 the brain of a dolphin. The part of the brain concerned with smelling is shown in black. From this we can see that the armadillo has a much greater sense of smell than a dog, and that the dolphin can smell very little indeed

and our sense of touch, smell and taste, we provide the brain with information on what is going on around us. The brain sorts out all these messages and in turn "tells" our muscles what movements to make. In times of emergency or when something happens to the body which requires quick countermeasures, as, for instance, when you are stung by an insect, the brain is bypassed. This prevents any loss of valuable time and the body can defend itself at once.

The sight and smell of a cup of coffee is passed to the brain, which then sends out messages to various parts of the body—for instance, to the mouth and arm

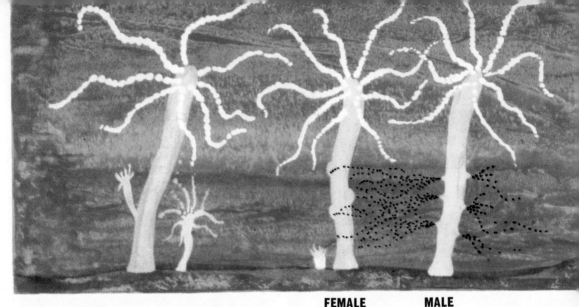

FEMALE   MALE

We said earlier that simple animals and plants can reproduce by splitting into two. We saw this happening in the case of amoebae, but even more complicated organisms, for instance Hydra, will also "grow" new organisms. These will eventually separate themselves from the parent and start life by themselves. But sometimes Hydra will produce *sex cells*, that is, special cells which can produce new organisms. Bulges appear on its sides which carry two different kinds of sex cells: *egg cells* and *sperms*. The sperms are set free and are able to move. If one of them finds an egg cell, usually in another Hydra, it will enter it and mix with the egg substance. This is called *fertilization* and in this way new organisms are brought into existence, for each fertilized egg cell will give birth to a new Hydra. The process of reproducing by means of sex cells is called *sexual reproduction*.

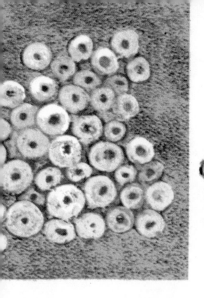

Frogs reproduce sexually. The female lays a great number of eggs. The male adds his sperms and so fertilizes some of the eggs. A fertilized egg splits again and again, grows into a tadpole and eventually the tadpole changes into a frog.

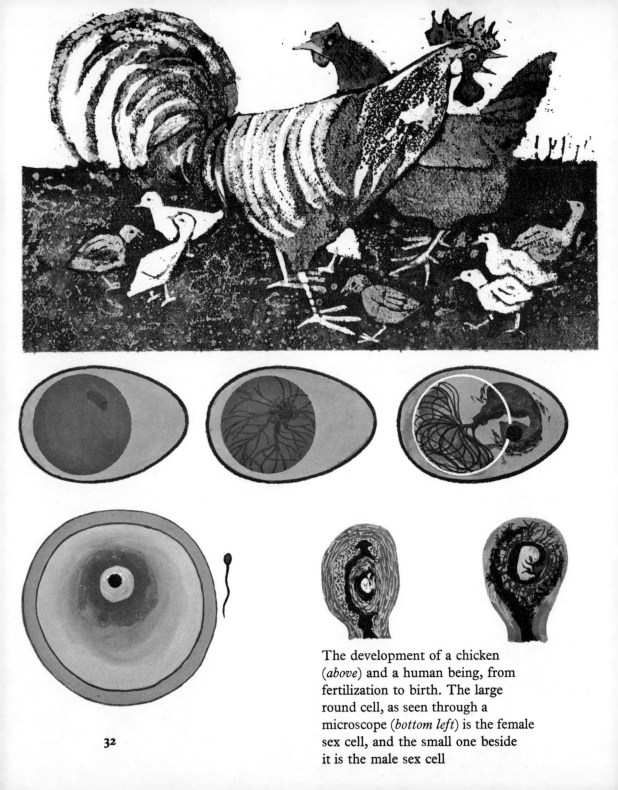

The development of a chicken (*above*) and a human being, from fertilization to birth. The large round cell, as seen through a microscope (*bottom left*) is the female sex cell, and the small one beside it is the male sex cell

This seems to work very well in the water but on land the female egg cells would be dried up long before they could be joined by sperms. In land animals, therefore, the sperm must fertilize the egg cell while the egg cell is still inside the body of the female. After this the fertile eggs may be laid and hatched outside the body, as with reptiles and birds, or they may remain in the body of the mother and develop there, the young being born at a later stage. This is what happens in man, dogs, cats and all the related animals called *mammals*, that is, animals which feed their young on their own milk.

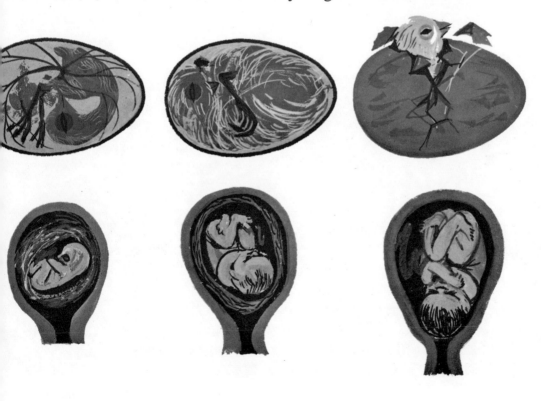

The earliest living things on the Earth were probably minute organisms living without oxygen. Later, microscopic green plants came to be formed in the oceans, which released free oxygen from the water, and the more complicated animals and plants developed. Gradually, in the course of many hundreds of millions of years, new types of living organisms have developed from older forms. Many types which existed in the past are

560 MILLION YEARS AGO

250 MILLION YEARS AGO

no longer found, that is, they have become *extinct*. But to understand this process properly we must look again at the cell.

125 MILLION YEARS AGO

50 MILLION YEARS AGO

How cells divide:

1 Cell at rest
2 Chromosomes become
   visible. Each one is
   split in two but the two
   halves are held together
   in the middle
3 Chromosomes shorten
   and thicken
4 Fibres appear
5 Chromosomes divide
6 Chromosomes move
   apart
7 Chromosomes form
   into two groups
8 A wall is formed
   between the two groups.
   There are now two cells
   instead of one

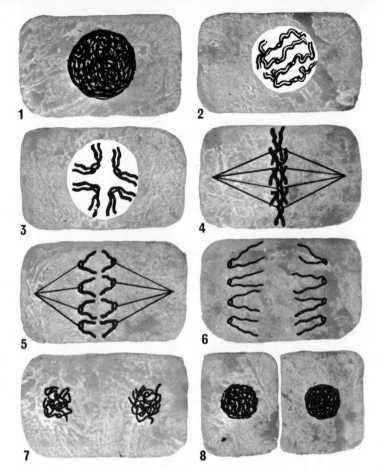

When a cell is about to divide, the nucleus can be seen to contain *chromosomes*. These pictures show what happens to the chromosomes when a cell splits. You can see that the new cell will have the same number of chromosomes as the old cell, so that all the cells of an organism have the same number of chromosomes. The cells of different organisms, plants or animals, have a definite number of chromosomes. The cells of human beings for instance, have 23 pairs of chromosomes, 46 in all. The cells of the shrimp have 254 chromosomes.

What happens when an egg cell joins up with a sperm to form a new cell? If each sex cell had the same number of chromosomes as ordinary cells, the new cell would have twice the number of chromosomes as it should have. That is why the cells that produce sex cells split in such a way that each sex cell contains single and not paired chromosomes. A sex cell therefore contains only half the number of chromosomes of an ordinary cell. When egg cell and sperm join to form a new cell, the chromosomes pair up and the new cell will contain the same number of chromosomes as the rest of the cell of the organism.

How sex cells are produced:

1 Chromosomes appear. They are not split
2 Chromosomes form pairs
3 Each pair splits
4 Fibres appear
5 Chromosomes move apart and form two groups
6 Dividing wall forms
7 and 8 New cells divide again
9 Four new cells have formed where there was originally one. However, each has only half the number of chromosomes of the original cell

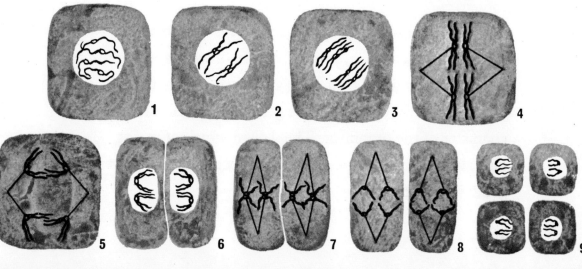

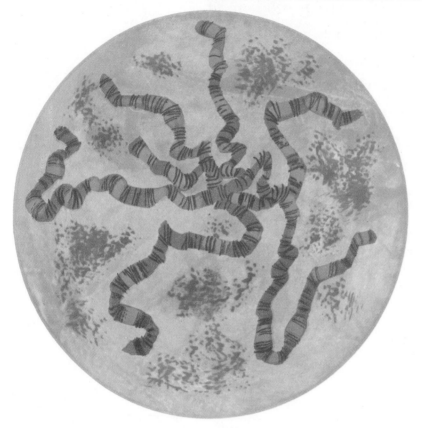

   The chromosomes contain *nucleic acids* which make up
structures called *genes,* and these control what goes on inside
the cell. When a cell splits, the genes are exactly copied and
passed on to the new cell. The genes determine the
character of the organism. The way in which offspring
take after their parents—*heredity*—depends on the pattern of
genes in the sex cells.

Sometimes, for accidental reasons, genes are not copied exactly, or they may be altered by certain chemicals like mustard gas, or by the action of X-rays or atomic radiation. When that happens the young animal which develops after fertilization may be affected in some way for good or ill. This gene change is called mutation, and the organism affected by a mutation is called a *mutant*.

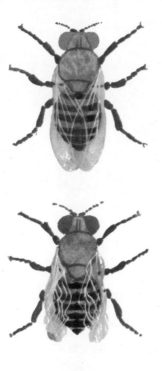

(*Left*) Mutants of the fruit fly, showing different eye colors and wings, and (*above*) mutant wheat

About a hundred years ago the peppered moth found in
England was light in color, but there was also a darker kind,
a mutant. The darker moth was not so successful as the lighter
kind and was not found very often. In the industrial areas of
England today, the situation is different: the darker moth
seems to be thriving while the light-colored one is not doing
so well, and only a few can be seen. The reason is that industry
has changed the color of the countryside and especially the
color of tree trunks. Birds feeding on moths would have

overlooked the light-colored moth on the tree trunk of a
hundred years ago, while the dark moth would have stood out
considerably and would have been eaten. But on the grimy
tree trunks of a highly industrialized countryside the light
moth will fall prey to the birds, while most dark ones will
survive. The mutation of the original peppered moth was a
change for the better, because conditions favored it. We can
say that the dark peppered moth was selected by nature for
survival; we call this process *Natural Selection.*

41

This kind of change may also occur on a larger scale and alter the appearance of an animal. The earliest horses, which lived between seventy and forty million years ago, were about the same size as greyhounds. Between then and recent times, changes have occurred in the form of the skull and brain, the teeth and in the bones of the foot. What causes these changes?

The early horses fed on twigs, leaves and shoots of plants. Their feet were used to the soft ground of forests. But between twenty and ten million years ago, the climate of North America became drier and the vast forests in which the early horses

lived gave way to grass-covered prairies. Horses with teeth better suited for grazing then appeared. Chewing grass soon wears down teeth and the more recent, grass-eating horses have teeth which are both longer and harder than those of the earlier horses. They also have longer legs and strong hoofs to enable them to run far and fast over the hard ground of the prairie.

These changes did not come about suddenly but by a series of mutations spread over millions of years. The only horses to survive were ones that could make the best of these conditions.

This development of new types from old is called *evolution*, and the man who did most to show that it occurred was Charles Darwin (1809–1882). He realized that small differences in living things would give some a better chance of surviving and leaving offspring.

In the face of bitter criticism, Darwin carefully collected facts which left no reasonable doubt about his theory of evolution.

Some mutations can be very useful to man. Seedless oranges are a mutant which would have died out if left to themselves because they could not have reproduced. But to us such oranges are preferable to the normal kind and growers increased their numbers by taking cuttings. The short-legged sheep in this picture is also a mutant, and some sheep farmers breed this type of sheep because it cannot jump over fences and is easier to manage.

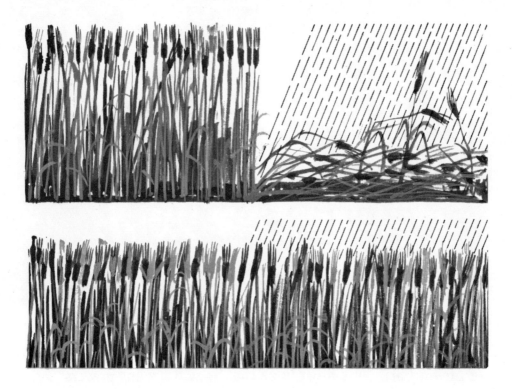

Until now barley could not be grown in countries where rainfall is heavy at harvest time. The heavy rain beats down the barley and causes great losses. Now atomic scientists have produced a new, short-stemmed kind of barley, by treating barley seeds with atomic radiation and bringing about mutation. This kind of barley can stand up to heavy weather and can be grown in many areas of the world where it could not have thrived before. All these mutations happened because of some changes to the genes in the sex cells.

Man, with his improved understanding of the chemistry of life, is now in a position to influence the future development of life on Earth. We must hope that he will use his powers wisely, growing better crops for food, and preserving interesting plants and animals which otherwise might die out.

Scientists investigating the secrets of life are still faced with many baffling problems. *Biochemists* are steadily advancing toward a better knowledge of what goes on inside cells, and we may reasonably hope that many important problems, for instance the causes and cure of cancer, will in time be solved. In cancer, some cells seem to change and get out of control, and grow in a way which damages other cells, and we need to know how they come to do this.

Soon astronauts will be on their way to the moon and planets, and they must be kept alive during their flights. Other planets in our solar system are not suitable for human life, but Mars may have living things of some kind. Men might live on Mars if they could use space suits with an oxygen supply. They could perhaps take simple plants with them and grow them under plastic domes which would trap oxygen given off by the plants. Food might also be produced in this way. There is no shortage of fascinating problems for the modern biologist to solve.

Some of the new words which you have read in this book.

Amoeba. One kind of single-celled animal.

Atoms. The smallest units of chemical elements.

Bacteria. The smallest truly living things.

Biochemist. A chemist who studies the chemistry of living organisms.

Carbohydrates. Sugar, starch and similar chemical compounds. They consist of carbon, hydrogen and oxygen.

Cellulose. A carbohydrate forming the walls of plant cells.

Chloroplast. A granule in a plant cell, containing chlorophyll.

Chlorophyll. The green coloring-matter of plants.

Compound microscope. A microscope containing two or more separate lenses.

Chromosomes. Rod-like or thread-like structures in the nucleus. They carry the genes.

Cytoplasm. Substance of a cell, excluding the nucleus.

Egg cells. Female sex cells.

Electron microscope. An instrument for producing very highly magnified detailed pictures of minute objects.

Extinct. No longer existing.

Evolution (of organisms). The theory that all existing living things have descended from earlier types by a series of changes.

Enzymes. Special proteins present in cells which help to bring about the chemical reactions necessary for living.

Fertilization. Joining together of egg cell and sperm.

Genes. Nucleic acids in chromosomes. They control heredity.

Heredity. Passing on of features from one generation to another.

Mammals. Animals, including man, which feed their young on their own milk, and have hair on their skins.

Microscope. An instrument for producing magnified images of objects.

Microscopic. Too small to be seen with the naked eye.

Molecule. Two or more atoms joined together.

Mutant. An organism which differs from its parent(s) because of the change in one or more genes.

Nucleus. Part of a cell containing chromosomes.

Natural selection. Survival of those types of organisms which are best able to live and produce offspring in the surroundings in which they happen to be.

Nucleic acids. Large molecules made up of carbon, hydrogen, oxygen, nitrogen and phosphorus. They control many of the processes which go on inside cells, and are important for cell division and heredity.

Organism. A living thing.

Photosynthesis. Building up of complicated chemicals from carbon dioxide and water, by means of the energy of sunlight.

Proteins. Substances with large molecules, built up of carbon, hydrogen, oxygen, nitrogen and sometimes other elements.

Protoplasm. Substance of a cell.

Protozoa. Microscopic animals.

Sex cells. Cells which can join together (male and female) and start the production of a new organism .

Sexual reproduction. Production of offspring from a fertilized egg, formed by joining of male and female sex cells.

Skeleton. Hard, supporting structure of an animal body.

Sperm. A male sex cell.

Tissue. A collection of cells of some particular kind.